They whispered to you...

"You can not withstand the storm"

Until you whisper back...

"I am the storm"

I'm so proud of you danny for realising what you've been involved in... It's the first step to recovery and claiming your soul back.

love
x

The Little Book of Narcissist Quotes

Alice Little

The advice in this book is given in good faith based on the experiences of the author. The reader should not rely on it alone and is advised to seek further professional help. Any use of information in this book is at the reader's discretion and risk. Neither the author nor the publisher can be held responsible for any loss, claim or damage arising out of the use, or misuse, of the suggestions made, the failure to take medical advice or for any material on third party websites.

All rights reserved. No part of this publication may be reproduced, stored in a retrieval system, or transmitted, in any form or by any means, electronic, mechanical, photocopying, recording or otherwise, without the prior written permission of the publisher/author. Contents remain the property of the author.

All quotes in this book are by the author Alice Little and may not be used without the permission of the author.

Copyright © 2018 Alice Little

ABOUT THE AUTHOR

The author is a survivor of parental narcissistic abuse and abuse by other narcissists as an adult. She has over 30 years experience in various self development therapies. As a survivor of going No Contact with her family of origin, she now advises others on parental narcissistic abuse, going no contact, and healing from trauma as an adult caused by emotional abuse.

ACKNOWLEDGMENTS

I could not have created this book without the help of my husband who has patiently helped me to edit every word I write. Someone who has been an emotional support throughout my journey of recovery. He reminds me that even after a lifetime of narcissistic abuse, that unconditional love is possible, and that I deserve to be loved, and to be able to love another who is not only, not a narcissist, but is also everything they never were.

INTRODUCTION

Narcissists, don't you just love them! They ruin your life and take the best years from you. Then you spend the rest of your time, time you could have been enjoying yourself and just living, on trying to learn about *their* disorder. Just so you won't be fooled again. More time and attention given to the narcissist.

If your parents were narcissists you were nicely set up and brainwashed on how to meet a narcissist, without even knowing it! However, even if you had decent parents, still then, you can be conned by the narcissist.

By the time you finally wake up and realise that the reason you feel so mad is not that you are mad, but that the narcissists were, it is too late. More time in therapy. Even more losses arise as you move away from them and their 'flying monkeys' - the bully gang. People who you may have thought of as your friends, and even your own family, can become entangled in the narcissist's web, the narcissists very own hench team, while you end up alone.

Then when you finally go No Contact with a narcissist, usually after many years (we tend to stay a long time before waking up), you find out that most of the people you knew were also narcissists. Even your best friend can turn round and abuse you if the narcissist has started a smear campaign against you.

To get their revenge they will turn your children against you, financially abuse you and leave you with nothing, while they carry on as if nothing happened and then continue to flourish with a new replacement slave. It is so absurd that you have to laugh. Yet mostly we end up crying.

I have written this book of quotes based on many years of using my pen to heal myself and fight back against Narcissistic Abuse. I chose a pen rather than any other sharp instrument because that's who I am, a peaceful sort.

I hope you will find this book of good use on your journey of recovery from this very damaging, often hidden, type of abuse.

To use this book you can either read it from cover to cover, or think of a question and open a page randomly and see what is written. Maybe it will be just what you need to hear! Carry it with you everywhere, as a reminder, in case you forget how bad it actually was. However you use it I hope that it heals you, educates you, inspires you and even makes you smile.

> **THE NARCISSIST WILL ALWAYS HELP YOU QUENCH YOUR THIRST, BY PASSING YOU A GLASS OF SALT WATER.**

THE NARCISSIST'S IDEA OF HELP

Look at this quote, isn't that just the truth!

We even used to take the water from them, thank them, and then drink it because they told us it was just water. Then one day we taste it and realise it is not just water but is actually salt water. We aren't going to drink it anymore because it will not quench our thirst. Yet when we hand back the glass of salt water to them they try to 'gaslight' us by denying it is salt water. That we must be imagining it. They will even get other people to taste it and they too will say 'No its just water, you must be imagining it'. We used to believe it once, their crazy world, then we wake up and get the hell out of that mad place.

> NARCISSISTIC ABUSE LEAVES YOU FEELING PSYCHOLOGICALLY HOMELESS.

PSYCHOLOGICALLY HOMELESS

When you live with a narcissist you get to live in their crazy world. So when you leave you feel psychologically homeless. You are not at home in your head and feel that someone evicted you. It is a strange feeling that you have, a disconnection from yourself.

It is as if the narcissist removed your own mind and replaced it with theirs. They told you that everything you said, did or felt was no good and you believed it. In doing so they told you they were superior and that everything they said, do and feel is what you should also be feeling.

When you leave them you may actually become homeless on a material level as well, and you will also become psychologically homeless, because they took away your ability to be 'you'. They destroyed you by telling you that you didn't exist. When you were with them you probably felt invisible anyway.

Then you have to spend the rest of your years trying to mentally get home to yourself. You have to learn to inhabit your mind, body and soul because you have been evicted from all three by the narcissist. We lose so much in our interactions with narcissists that we become psychologically homeless.

> OVER TIME YOU REALISE THAT THE ONLY THING NARCISSISTS HAD TO OFFER WAS CHARISMA, AND EVEN THAT WAS FAKE!

NARCISSISTS CAN BE VERY CHARISMATIC

It was like being conned by the worst kind of salesperson when you met them, wasn't it? They sold you something you didn't really want - *them*! They did sell you something you needed, love, but that was empty words. The actions didn't match. Not long after they had hooked you in good and proper, the mask started to drop.

They can be very charismatic, they have to be otherwise you wouldn't touch them with a barge pole. I prefer to think of them as stage hypnotists because you could not have been sold this lie unless you were hypnotised.

Under the sway of the swinging solid gold watch they dangled in front of your eyes, you thought they were who they said they were. I'm sure you have watched stage hypnotists haven't you? Where they get people to believe they are ducks and they even quack. They don't even remember when they wake up what they were doing. Narcissists use charisma as a form of hypnosis.

> PEOPLE CAN'T TAKE TOO MUCH TRUTH BUT THEY HAVE A LOT OF TIME FOR LIES AND FAKERY.

BELIEVING THE NARCISSIST'S LIES

Can you remember when you were with the narcissist and refused to believe the truth of who they were? Even when people tried to tell you who they were you would not believe it. Yet when you left and tried to tell everyone how rotten they actually were, no one else believed you either!

Narcissists are good at creating fake. They are like a big movie company selling you a dream life in a film. Then the film ends. Yet while you were watching it you were in it, believed it was real. When it ends you are left holding your popcorn crying into the bucket over something that wasn't even real.

Yes, people would rather believe lies and fakery because it helps them avoid how crap everything really is. They would rather believe the narcissist is the great person they made out they were than admit the truth that their life has been a lie. It is a sad story we create when we fall for a fake.

> AS NARCISSISTIC ABUSE SURVIVORS WE HAD EVERYTHING STOLEN FROM US. WE GET SO USED TO HAVING THAT DONE TO US THAT WE OWN NOTHING. WE GIVE EVERYTHING AWAY FREELY WHILE THE NARCISSIST WILL CARRY ON STEALING OUR STUFF. WE NEED TO START OWNING WHAT IS OURS AND FEEL NO SHAME IN DOING SO.

WE GIVE EVERYTHING AWAY FOR FREE

You will leave with nothing. While they will carry on just as before but with a new replacement slave. While you struggle to mentally, physically and financially just get by, day by day, they will thrive.

Not content to leave you totally penniless and broken, they will still hound you for anything you do have left. No matter how little you have, they want you to be left with nothing!

Because we are generous and kind we get so used to giving everything away and not becoming attached to our stuff. The narcissist will help you feel you deserve nothing. To cope, you will shut off any feelings you have about ownership, and tell yourself you don't care but you do care. If you don't care now you will in the future, when you get your strength back, boy will you care!

Having to re-learn how to own things will be a new learning curve for you. You will be too embarrassed to put your name to anything, art, writing, houses, cars, you name it. While other narcissists will happily take your free stuff from you and even sell it. Meanwhile you will alleviate your guilt for existing by giving, but resentment will grow.

Why should we feel shameful for owning things? Put your name to something now and make it yours, before another narcissist drops by and steals everything again.

> A TRUTH ABOUT NARCISSISTS.......
> EVERYTHING THAT IS YOURS IS THEIRS. EVERYTHING THAT YOU OWN IN PARTNERSHIP IS THEIRS AND EVERYTHING THAT IS THEIRS IS THEIRS, NOT FOR SHARES.

EVERYTHING BELONGS TO THE NARCISSIST

When you meet a narcissist you will not know it at first but you are destined for loss. Any appearance of them sharing what they have is tinged with a huge price tag that you will have to pay in full. The things you shared, yours and theirs, were theirs all along. You will not know this until you leave because their sharing was based on your compliance to be controlled by them. Even that you will not see in full until it is too late. If you brought anything to the table, they will take it.

The narcissist does not see anything separate to them, only part of them. They have no boundaries with anyone, especially you and your stuff. They are particularly bad with personal space and they can't understand why you would want any. Meantime they demand pretty much all of the space.

When you split up, if you had a shared business, it's theirs, house, theirs, children, theirs. Everything belongs to them. So if you are still with them and you know that, start to stash away some money and a good plan for how to deal with the 'left with nothing' syndrome.

> The narcissist is like a crooked banker. A fictitous bank account is set up the minute you meet them. They will pay in heavy investments of help, care, money and gifts. Then they will charge you incredibly high interest, in the form of what you can offer to them as payback for their original investment. In the end they will call in the debt you owe when you are at your most broke. Then they will take off with the next investor (mug!) and leave you with nothing!

NARCISSISTS ARE JUST CROOKS

What's your dream? Or more like it, what is your need? If you have either, the narcissist predator will help you to fulfil these by offering you empty promises that you just can't resist. So enamored will you be by them that you will not see that they just want to torment you. You will be like a donkey following a carrot on a string it can't reach.

They will sell you a lie about themselves that seems too good to be true, it is! Run, if it's not too late. Once you are bewitched by these no-good charlatans they will empty, not only your bank account, but you. By the time they have run off with your stash you will be too bewildered to see that you were miss-sold an empty bank account by them.

The bank of narcissistic abuse never fills up, it needs constantly topping up. If you are with a narcissist you will always be empty of spirit and broken of heart. They are nothing but crooked bankers. What a bad investment they were!

> WHEN A DOOR CLOSES BEHIND YOU, WRITE ABOUT IT. THEN NAIL IT TIGHTLY SHUT SO THAT YOU ARE NEVER TEMPTED TO WALK THOUGH IT EVER AGAIN.

NEVER GO BACK!

Get the hammer and nails out now, you will need them. When you close the door on them and breathe a sigh of relief, even then, if they come knocking, you will be tempted to let them in. So strong is their hold on you that you forgot why you shut the door in the first place.

They will post cards and gifts through that door but you must not accept them. They pretend they have changed. All of a sudden the dream person you were longing for, imagined they were at first, has returned. Full of fancy phrases and empty promises, they only want you to come back to torment you.

Pin large notices on the back of this door, a set of rules to remind you why you ended this sham of a relationship, reminders of why you should not open it ever again.

> IT WAS THEIR CRAZY NOT MINE. I CHOSE SANITY AND LEFT!

IT WAS THEIR CRAZY NOT YOURS!

By the time you go No Contact you are half crazy. Led to the edge of a great abyss by the narcissist's craziness, you stopped just in time, and chose sanity. You look at how near you got to falling apart for good. Then you woke up one day and saw them for who they were, mentally ill people who were trying to mentally destroy you.

It is hard to believe that this person who you placed above you is nothing other than a fool. You start to see their craziness and in doing so see what danger you are in.

Being with them is like living with a torturer. Even if they don't lay a hand on you, their words stab like swords at your very being. It is difficult to pull out all the unkind words they placed inside you. They sit like a bomb waiting to go off at any moment.

It is hard to believe they are as you now truthfully see them. You so much don't want your life with them to have been a lie, a waste of time, a bad nightmare, but it was. All the time you thought you were crazy and now you know for sure, it was them.

> IT IS NOT AN ERROR IN YOUR MAKE UP, A FLAW IN YOUR CHARACTER, THAT YOU DON'T TRUST. IT IS A CLEVER, INTELLIGENT SYSTEM TO HELP YOU STAY AWAKE TO NARCISSIST PREDATORS.

NOT TRUSTING IS HEALTHY

When you were with a narcissist your world was turned upside down. They made you believe that what was crooked was straight and what was straight was crooked. You believed in lies and fakery. You fell for the con, the illusion. Now you are waking up to how the world actually works. You see you trusted too much, trusted the wrong people. Not trusting is normal. It is how you should have been before, checking trust, and not believing the mirage presented to you.

Humans are not trustworthy and there are predators around looking for those who are kind and trusting, like you. Animals have more discernment than humans. They are always alert to predators. Humans want to hang out and relax and not think about it, that is the point when they become vulnerable.

The only thing you have to do is start to be OK with not trusting, to accept it as the new you. Be proud that you don't trust, you are in a period where you are healing and you need to protect yourself. You are vulnerable. Over time things will change. You will stop seeing every person in the world as a narcissist and you will be able to relax a bit more.

> LIVING WITH A NARCISSIST MEANT WE HAD TO EAT OUR WORDS, SWALLOW OUR PRIDE, STUFF DOWN OUR FEELINGS, REMAIN INVISIBLE, NOT TAKE UP ROOM, MELT INTO THE BACKGROUND, WALK ON EGGSHELLS, ALL IN ORDER TO AVOID ABUSE THAT WAS UNAVOIDABLE. SO YES, WE DO HAVE POST TRAUMATIC STRESS DISORDER!

WALKING ON EGGSHELLS

After some time with the narcissist you get to realise just how traumatised you have become. You dare not say the wrong thing, do the wrong thing, or look the wrong way.
It is impossible to guess what exactly they want because it does not matter how hard you try, your best is never good enough.

You turn into a 'people pleaser' a narcissist's lackey. There to do their bidding just to keep the peace. The narcissist meanwhile wants you to become emotional so they can get their feed. If you don't become emotional they will provoke you even further.

You start to change your character and so, to the outside world, it looks like you are just a crabby, miserable loser. Meanwhile the narcissist is dining on your depression and laughing with your mates behind your back. It is not until after you leave that you see they were all in on it, friends and anyone else's lives they touched. They poisoned everyone around you. If you are lucky you might have an ally that will help you but most survivors end up ditching everyone.

The narcissist will carry on gorging on your demise and flourishing while you run off with nothing but your broken self.

> AFTER NO CONTACT.
> AFTER NARCISSISTIC ABUSE.
> EVEN THEN YOU WILL CRY AND
> GRIEVE. IT IS NORMAL BUT YOU
> WILL GET LITTLE SYMPATHY.
> SO HERE, I'M SENDING YOU
> SOME. I KNOW HOW IT ALL FEELS.
> I'M SO SORRY IT HAPPENED TO
> YOU TOO.

NO ONE WILL UNDERSTAND WHAT YOU ARE GOING THROUGH

After, and even during, life with a narcissist, it is most likely that no one will understand what you have been through or what you are going through. The narcissist's abuse is often hidden by both you and others. Even close friends may not have seen what was happening to you. So when you leave they think you just had a tiff and they may try to get you back to your abuser.

They think you are over reacting and you need help. They don't know that you now have Complex Post Traumatic Stress Disorder caused by prolonged and repeated abuse. It is even worse that the abuse was possibly hidden. You yourself even feel like you are going crazy.

Believe me this will not last forever! You will start to see, once you have gone No Contact, that it was, in fact, *they* that were crazy. They took you into their world and tried to break you down. You will start to get back your confidence, though it won't be overnight, and you will see exactly what you did not see then. Systematic abuse.

I know how that feels, I was once there too. But now I'm out the other side, thriving. I am here to tell you that if no one else understands, I do. I'm so sorry it happened to you too!

> NO ONE UNDERSTANDS WHAT IT IS LIKE TO BE A FUGITIVE FROM YOUR PAST. TO BE FREE YET HAVE ALL THE NORMAL FREEDOMS THAT OTHERS ENJOY, REMOVED.

YOU ARE FREE YET YOU STILL FEEL CAGED

The utter relief you feel when you finally leave them and go No Contact. You sit down and relax in the peace that their lack of presence brings. Then you find out that they seem to have camped out in that space between your ears. Even though they are no longer there you can still hear them dishing out the orders and putting you down. You thought it would all end the day you left but instead find that it continues. They are like a permanent ghost haunting you. Who needs to be afraid of spooks when you have these people inhabiting your space like a disembodied voice?

You have gone No Contact but still they call you, drop by and stay in your life. If you moved away and tried to hide they will send their sniffer dogs, 'flying monkeys', in the form of anyone you knew to hound you out. These people who you may have once thought of as close are now acting on behalf of your worst enemy. Some friends they were!

ANYONE WHO SHAMES SURVIVORS OF TRAUMA AND ABUSE FOR NOT HEALING, IS A PERSON WHO HAS NO COMPASSION FOR LIFE'S SUFFERING.

THE SHAME OF NOT HEALING

You are supposed to heal, get better, get over it, but you feel you aren't. People keep telling you to get a life, move on, be happy, but you can't. So you feel like a failure. Yet none of these people who tell you you should be healing have any knowledge of your personal life experience. If they did they would know that healing is an individual thing. They would also know that healing sometimes means just finding a way to cope with the damage that has been done to you.

Healing is not a destination, it is a path, the path of life. It is like walking through a valley and reaching a plateau, then climbing a mountain and coming back down again. It comes in waves up and down. Yet even this up and down is a healing.

You will find over time that you have healed and moved on, it's just that you may not have noticed. So intent were you on healing that you forgot to look up and notice that you had walked right out of a dark forest and into the light.

Let no one shame you for not healing. You are healing. At your own pace and in your own way. Let yourself be the judge of how well you are doing not others. One day you will see that you came through it all. It may not be perfect, but it's perfect for you. Compared to where you were everything is perfect. Celebrate that!

> I DON'T DO THE RUNNING ANYMORE. I LIKE TO MEET IN THE MIDDLE WHERE BOTH SIDES HAVE MADE EQUAL PACE TOWARDS EACH OTHER. NOW, INSTEAD, I STAND IN MY OWN SPACE WITH CONFIDENCE KNOWING THAT THOSE WHO SHOULD BE IN MY LIFE WILL WALK TOWARDS ME.

NO MORE RUNNING AFTER THEM

Did you notice how you did a lot of running after people, mostly narcissists? How you tried to get people to like you by being more jolly, more entertaining and being a doormat. Were you the one who always called? What about when you met new people did you rush towards them with outstretched hands while they looked at you as if you were weird? It was impossible trying to be liked and you *were* weird.

Most people prefer those who are confident in their own space, those with a slight bit of mystery, not someone who divulges their whole life story in one sitting. It was not that you were friendly, though you wanted to appear that way, it was that you wanted to be liked. That's why you tried so hard. That is why the narcissists noticed you. They saw you were open and trusting and kind. 'I can use that', they thought. So when others were not that friendly towards you, they were, and you never questioned it. You thought it meant that they liked you.

Now it is time to stand in your own space allowing others to walk towards you. To feel OK if they don't, knowing that the right people will appear in your life. Time to be confident with who you are. Some will like you, others not. Who do you want in your life? Not more narcissists. Concentrate on the relationship you have with yourself and all else will come right over time.

> LONELINESS IS SOMETHING THAT IS FELT WHEN ONE IS ALONE, BY ONESELF, NO ONE TO TURN TO. YET WHEN YOU LIVE WITH A NARCISSIST YOU WILL EXPERIENCE A LONELINESS THAT IS INDESCRIBABLE. IT IS AS IF THEY ERASE YOU, YOU BECOME INVISIBLE, NON EXISTANT.

THE LONELINESS OF NARCISSISTIC ABUSE

They erase you from life. Turn you into a shell of who you were. You could be sitting alone with them at a restaurant, and it would be as if you were not there. They look right through you, appear bored, and you feel as if it is you who has done something wrong.

Once they have you, unless they want something, they will just stop trying. You will not know what is wrong so you try harder, and all it gets you is anger and verbal abuse. It is as if you are trying to entertain a small toddler who won't stop crying, and the harder you try, the worse it gets. If you stop trying to please them they will accuse you of being sullen, miserable and even ungrateful.

When you are at home with them they will treat you even worse. Now it is as if you were in *their* castle. You will have to run after them as if you were their personal assistant. They are like little tyrants, despots of their own little fiefdom, which they control.

Loneliness almost does not describe the feeling of abandonment you experience while living with a Narcissist. 'Utter desolation' is a more appropriate description.

> THE NARCISSIST IS NOTHING OTHER THAN A STAGE HYPNOTIST. THEY HYPNOTISED YOU. YOU LISTENED TO THEIR WORDS, LOOKED INTO THEIR EYES AND DIDN'T SEE THE BODY CUES AND ANCHORS THEY WERE USING. ONCE YOU KNOW HOW HYPNOSIS WORKS YOU CAN LOOK BACK AND SEE HOW THEY DID IT. IT WAS JUST A STAGE TRICK.

THE NARCISSIST IS JUST A STAGE HYPNOTIST

You were hypnotised by the narcissist and once you understand how hypnotism works it all starts to make sense. Can you remember how gorgeous their voice was, the tone of it? Was it strong with rich warm chest notes, or soft and soothing? You may have been so enamored by their voice that you didn't even listen to what they were saying to you. Those subliminal words placed at just the right time, to get you interested, were carefully crafted, maybe used before on another victim before you.

Then when they were sure that the words and voice had entranced you, they anchored that with a carefully placed touch with their hands upon you. Bingo! You are now under the spell.

In stage hypnotism only the hypnotist can wake you up. It is the same with narcissists. Without even knowing it, they wake you up from your long sleep by their inability to keep up their facade. They become disappointed in you because you have sussed it out and are no longer compliant. In showing their real faces they clicked their finger and woke you up. It took you a while even though all the signs were there.

You are no longer a good subject for hypnosis so either you or the narcissist discard each other. They then go off in search of a new victim while you remain bewildered and wondering what had happened to you. Seeking to find out how hypnotism works enables you to never get caught again.

I WOULD RATHER LIVE ALONE OR AS AN OUTSIDER AND A MIS-FIT THAN LIVE IN THE MIND AND REALITY OF YET ANOTHER PSYCHOPATH. NOTHING COULD BE WORSE THAN THAT, EVEN LONELINESS.

THE LONELINESS OF LIVING WITH A NARCISSIST

You were alone when you were with them so could anything be worse than that? Living with a psychopath is dangerous for your health. They should come with a warning.

While you are under their spell they will take you into a world of crazy that is unlike anything you have ever experienced. It is they that are mentally ill, but by being with them it is you that will become mentally *illed*!

Even though they are abusive, covertly or overtly, still you can not live without them. It is as if they got under your skin and live in your mind. So if you are worried that in leaving them you will be alone and lonely, remind yourself how lonely you were when with them.

Let people think what they want, they did anyway, so give them something to talk about. Instead of worrying about loneliness think about how peaceful it will be without the narcissist ruining your every day. Imagine being able to do whatever you please without fear of abuse and put downs.

Much better to be alone than to live in the crazy mind and world of another psycho.

> ONCE YOU OUTDID YOUR USEFULNESS THEY REPLACED YOU FOR ANOTHER. ANOTHER CHEW TOY. ONCE YOU HAD BEEN BROKEN THAT IS. EVEN DOGS ARE KINDER TO THEIR CHEW TOYS.

THE NARCISSIST'S CHEW TOY

When you leave a narcissist you need not worry if they can live without you because they can. In fact a replacement was probably already waiting in the wings. If you remember how they groomed and tricked you, it is easy to imagine several other victims lining up too.

They will feign words telling you that they don't want you to leave, but they are empty words. They just want a victim, a dog's chew toy, something to help them stop grinding their teeth, to chew against, a tooth guard. They don't miss you, you are replaceable. Yet even when you have been replaced they still want you to hang around so they can have a collection of victims.

It is hard to believe that someone you loved can be so cold and uncaring. Yet the signs were there before you left, it's just that you didn't want to see them. It is often not until after you leave that you see how they got on with their life very well, while you stayed pining for them.

> WHEN YOUR LIFE HAS BEEN FILLED WITH PUT DOWNS, ABUSE, DEGRADATION, GASLIGHTING, BULLYING. WHEN YOU HAVE BEEN SO USED TO BEING INVISIBLE, NOT SEEN AND TIPTOEING AROUND THEM TO TRY TO AVOID ABUSE. AFTER THAT WHEN ANY GOOD THING HAPPENS, SOMEONE IS KIND, SUPPORT ARRIVES AND HAPPINESS IS FELT, IT IS HARD TO ACCEPT OR BELIEVE THAT IT IS FOR US. IT'S LIKE A POSTMAN KNOCKS WITH A GIFT FOR YOU AND YOU SAY 'OH NO! IT MUST BE FOR THE PERSON NEXT DOOR, NOT FOR ME, NEVER ME'.

NOT FOR ME!

We got so used to having our stuff taken by narcissists, or feeling that everything was theirs, that ownership of anything is embarrassing to us. If we paint a picture, we can't stand to be given money for it, so we devalue it by giving it away, feeling that that is being humble. If we have any talent whatsoever we give it away, give away our services for free. We devalue ourselves in every aspect of our lives.

So when someone actually values us, tells us we are worth something we tend to not believe them. Surely they don't mean it, it must be a lie.

If someone is genuinely kind to us we look away, look around the room for another person who they surely must be talking about. We don't feel we deserve anything good because we got so used to being told we were bad.

We send so much good stuff away when it comes knocking on our doors because we can't believe it is for us.

> WHEN THINGS START TO GO WELL FOR YOU, IT IS ONLY A MATTER OF TIME BEFORE THE LITTLE NARCISSIST BABIES TURN UP TO GRAB YOUR TOYS OFF YOU!

WHEN THINGS START TO GO WELL

When you get your life back on track and are doing well, even succeeding at something, it is as if we must let off some kind of radar to narcissists at that time because they come out of the woodwork to fleece us of it all. They see what we are doing and they want some of it, all of it. Many of us are so afraid of this happening, and so used to it, that we often don't fight back, we let them have it. Fighting for something had repercussions when you lived with a narcissist.

Narcissists know who they can steal from. They don't go for people who it would be difficult to take from. For those who are survivors of narcissistic abuse we know it must have been like taking sweets from a baby for them. We have to forgive ourselves for being so vulnerable. We gave away our things and we keep on doing it even after we have left.

There are always going to be narcissists coming along and trying to take whatever you have. Now we have to learn to say NO! This is mine!

> IF SOMEONE WHO HAS BEEN ABUSED CAN SHOW KINDNESS AND LOVE, THE REST OF THE WORLD HAS NO EXCUSE NOT TO.

WHY CAN'T EVERYONE JUST BE KIND?

Even those who have been abused can still be kind. Many were abused because they were kind. Narcissists trash those of us who have good hearts. No one else would put up with them.

We loved and cared for them and in return we got abuse, it doesn't add up. After we leave them we still remain kind and have a good heart, most of us. Some have been so broken by it that they shield their heart, becoming cold. We can't blame anyone for doing so. All of us may have experienced this phase of healing, self protection.

Yet if someone who has been so badly treated can be even a tiny bit kind to another being, the rest of the world has no excuse not to. The world needs kindness. Never give up on love.

> THE NARCISSIST WILL OFTEN SET UP FAKE MEETINGS WITH PEOPLE YOU DON'T WANT TO MEET. SOMEONE WHO YOU MAY NOT BE TALKING TO OR EVEN WANT TO KNOW AND OFTEN A CONTACT OF THE NARCISSIST. THEY WILL TELL EACH SIDE THAT THE OTHER ONE WANTS TO MEET THEM. NEITHER OF YOU WILL KNOW THAT YOU HAVE BEEN SET UP. THE REASON THEY DO THIS IS SO THEY CAN GET THEIR NARC FEED BY WATCHING YOU FEEL UNCOMFORTABLE WITH ONE OF THEIR FLYING MONKEYS. SETTING YOU UP FOR FURTHER ABUSE BECAUSE YOU THINK THIS OTHER PERSON WANTS TO BE YOUR FRIEND.

FLYING MONKEYS (gang of bullies!)

The narcissist in your life loves to play games. They will set up situations guaranteed to make you a laughing stock. It is their way of getting an emotional high, at the expense of another. They don't like to get their hands dirty so they set up a group of bullies to do it for them. These people are referred to as 'flying monkeys'.

One of their favourite things to do is to set up meetings in order for the victim to feel thoroughly uncomfortable. They will set up a meeting with someone who you do not like or do not talk to, maybe even a sibling. They will tell the other person that you want to meet them. Then they will tell you that the other person wants to meet you. Neither of you have actually said this at all.

One of the worst examples is perhaps when the ex narc says that their new partner wants to meet you. They, meanwhile, think you want to meet them and instant rivalry is formed. Or on another scale, a useful flying monkey for the narcissist is created by making them your friend.

The meeting will be a disaster for you and a triumph for the narc. Neither party will even say 'oh I hear you wanted to meet me' and be suspicious because they will believe that the meeting was all true. Often it is not until much later that you see through this set up and work out how it was done to you.

> NO IS NOT SOMETHING THAT NEEDS AN EXPLANATION. IT IS A SENTENCE ALL ON ITS OWN. IT HAS ONE MEANING AND IT DOES'T MEAN YES. IT REQUIRES NO OTHER WORDS TO EXPLAIN IT, NO EXCUSES OR REASONS WHY A NO IS GIVEN.
> NO MEANS NO

LET YOUR NO BE NO

We have to learn to say no and mean it after abuse because we see how we said yes in so many ways when we meant to say no. We gave our time freely when we needed to be doing other things. We cancelled things we wanted to do in order to please the narcissist. In fact so afraid of them were we, that 'no' was never a word we spoke, for fear of more abuse.

When we give in to a tyrant's needs they just become more demanding and we find that even saying yes is not enough. Yet as soon as we say no, firmly, the boot will come down on us. If you ever started to stand up to your narcissist you will see that they got quickly bored with you, or angry. Their intensity of abuse increased or they found a new model to discard you for.

Once we go no contact we become more knowledgeable about how narcissists operate and we should also apply that to ourselves, how we operate. We have to start to say no to things, testing it out in small ways first. The more we learn to say no, and say yes to ourselves, the more empowered we will become.

It is a new skill which will take time. We are only afraid to say no because we have no self confidence that the other will not persuade us to change the no to a yes, or abuse us. Try it out today. Say no to something you don't want. You will soon get used to it.

> SENSITIVE, TOUCHY, DEFENSIVE, EASILY SPOOKED, AFRAID, PARANOID, HYPERVIGILANT, DISTRUSTING, ISOLATED, EDGY, JUMPY, HIGHLY STRUNG, ADDICTIONS, MENTAL ILLNESS, ONE OR MORE PHYSICAL ILLNESSES. JUST A FEW OF THE UNWANTED GIFTS A NARCISSIST LEAVES YOU WITH. ADD YOU OWN!

NARCISSISTS MAKE YOU ILL

Until you leave a narcissist you will not realise just how ill they made you. You get so used to your predicament when you are with them that you think you are just an ill person. Many people take to their beds and never come out. This may be their last bastion of control and the sheer exhaustion of being abused by a narcissist.

Your mental health will have suffered greatly and instead of others having sympathy with you they will just think you are weird or overacting. It was just a break up so 'get over it'! Yet you can't get over it and that is the hardest part to come to terms with. It is like no other feeling that you ever had, this sickness of mind and body that will not leave.

If the narcissist was one of your parents it is even more difficult because you may feel that you can not leave them, just like any other relationship. They are family after all. If someone is abusing you, no matter who they are, or what relationship they are to you, if you can not make it right by sensible dialogue then you owe them nothing. Your mental health is more important.

It will not be until well after you leave a narcissist that you see the damage they have done. You wake up from your long sleep and start to see the truth. It was they who made you ill and you can clearly see how they did it. Then you can start to have compassion for yourself. You deserve it after all you have been through.

> THEY GET TO LIVE THE LIFE THEY TAKE FROM YOU.

A LIFE LOST

Going no contact means that you lose your life, as you knew it. Meanwhile there is a good chance that the narcissist will carry on like before. Their life staying the same, while yours is left destroyed. They replace you with another and mostly don't even notice you have gone. You will be the one crying, not them.

It is not easy to see from a distance, the narcissist living the life you were evicted from. They may be living in the home you had, spending the money you shared and even steal your children from you.

The friends that you had together may become their friends while you end up with none. The narcissist wants to see you suffer for leaving them, and they will usually do it in an area which they had the most control of when you left them.

You can't afford to let them see you falling apart, even if you have to fake it. Eventually you will not need to fake it, it will be real. Getting yourself together again will be your revenge. Then you can just look at their life knowing that they aren't really happy because narcissists can never be happy and content, ever.

> IT WAS THEIR CRAZY NOT MINE. I CHOSE SANITY AND LEFT!

NO CONTACT

When you are with a narcissist you will feel that you are crazy. They take you into a world that feels out of control. Your emotions seem to be on overdrive. Welcome to the crazy world of narcissists.

It is not until you have left, gone no contact, that you will see just how crazy it all was. They made you believe that the crooked was straight and the straight was crooked. You doubted everything you thought or felt and instead took on the feelings of the narcissist. You entered their crazy world and merged with them. You became a mirror for them. When the mirror no longer reflected the image they wanted to see of themselves, when a few truths were spoken, they tired of you. By that time you were truly feeling as low as you can get.

The good news is that after you leave you get curious about these people and you want to know how you got fooled by them. So you educate yourself. Wouldn't the narcissist be so pleased that you were spending even more time thinking about them!

Then the light goes on, and because you are no longer in their world you start to create your own. You realise the truth that it wasn't you that was crazy, but them. It is such a profound healing moment. The moment you disconnect from them and get yourself back. Sane again!

> YOU ARE NOT MAD.
> YOU ARE RECOVERING FROM TRAUMA.
> MAD PEOPLE ABUSED YOU.

YOU ARE RECOVERING FROM TRAUMA

You have finally discovered that you are not mad. Mad people are the ones who abused you. Just knowing this is a big step. Because their abuse is repeated over and over again it creates within us trauma and Complex Post Traumatic Stress Disorder. We leave and survive but now we have to deal with trauma. We do not know what is wrong with us, we still feel a little crazy. We are jumpy and triggered by all sorts of things. We don't trust and the world around us seems like a very different place.

We now have to start looking after ourselves and it is unusual. Before this, all we thought about was pleasing and looking after them. Trauma makes us have to take care of ourselves, it demands it. Often there is a period of isolation when all we want to do is to be alone, it is normal.

Building up our self-esteem and starting to care for ourselves will make us stronger for when we decide to return to life. The world is a different place now, as a trauma survivor. You have skills you did not have before and you know truths about life and people that you did not know either. It is as if you were reborn. It is a joy to know that you were not crazy and you strive to learn how not to let crazy people ever abuse you again. Healing begins.

> THE ONE THING THAT YOU CAN RELY ON WITH NARCISSISTS IS THAT THEY ARE PREDICTABLE. ONCE YOU WORK OUT THEIR PATTERN OF BEHAVIOUR YOU CAN'T REALLY TAKE THEM SERIOUSLY EVER AGAIN. IN FACT, YOU MAY EVEN BE SLIGHTLY AMUSED BY THEM.

PREDICTABLE NARCISSISTS

Narcissists are very predictable once you know their game. They give away signs, follow similar patterns in relationships, do the same old things repeatedly. When you are with them you don't notice their game so much as when you leave, then you can clearly see the pattern.

It is very empowering to know finally how they operate, how they got to you. At that point you are then able to see other narcissists at work and say 'no thank you'. Their past relationships will tell you a lot about them. They are big into blaming previous partners, it was never their fault.

Everything they did and said was a lie to manipulate you and you fell for it. Even when your instincts told you otherwise you doubted it because the truth is so painful, they never loved you.

There are so many variations of narcissists and the type you are with may not totally match who you thought narcissists were. Not all narcissists are noisy, bold and brash. Some are quiet and shy, putting you off guard if you are not familiar with them. Study all the types just in case you are fooled again by a quiet one. Don't listen to the hard luck stories the quiet one's tell you to hook you in and don't fall for the false charisma of a showy narc.

> CAN YOU REMEMBER WHEN YOU WERE WITH THE NARCISSIST AND YOU REFUSED TO BELIEVE WHO THEY WERE? EVEN WHEN PEOPLE TRIED TO TELL YOU WHO THEY WERE YOU STILL DID NOT BELIEVE IT. YET WHEN YOU LEFT THEM AND TRIED TO TELL OTHERS JUST HOW ROTTEN THEY ACTUALLY WERE, NO ONE ELSE WOULD BELIEVE IT EITHER!

THEY TELL YOU WHO THEY ARE BUT YOU IGNORED IT

Very early on there would have been signs telling you who they were. You would have ignored them in order to make them fit the ideal you wanted. They gave you that ideal and told you a lie about who they were. You were kind and trusting, that's why they picked you, so they could keep up their false sense of who they are. They can not stand to admit to all their faults.

When you finally start to see who they are and how they have been abusing you, then you try to tell others. Those others have also possibly been fooled by them too. You even kept it secret, how they were indoors, away from other's eyes. It can feel like there is no one to turn to.

Then you realise that the person you really need to believe you, is you. You see how you doubt the truth of how it was even when you leave. You create a rosy, romantic picture of them and leave out all the bad bits too, just like the narcissist did. It is you that you need to convince, only you, then everything will fall into place. You can start to trust yourself at last.

> AFTER NO CONTACT, FOR SOME SURVIVORS, IT IS LIKE SOLITARY CONFINEMENT IN THEIR OWN HOME. WHILE THE NARCISSIST ROAMS FREE AS A BIRD.

THE ISOLATION OF NO CONTACT

There is no doubt about it that no contact with a narcissist creates isolation and often loneliness. As an act of self protection survivors often choose to stay away from people due to not trusting. The very fact that you have left a narcissist often means that you lose the life you had and the people you knew and you are therefore thrust into a life alone.

The isolation can feel enforced and impossible to get out of but over time it lessens. Isolating after narcissistic abuse helps with the healing process. It gives you time to get to know yourself again. The time you spend away from life can also give you the space to study narcissism and can allow you time to arm yourself with some valid education about narcissist predators before you enter the world again.

Most people never get to spend this time alone, with themselves, because the whole world is running away from this very thing. Once you grow accustomed to the isolation you will start to value your time alone, start to be comfortable and happy with your own company. What better person could there be than someone who is happy in their own skin.

Don't let others rush you into getting back into the world too quickly, you will know when it is time for you. By then you will be re-entering life as another person, another you. A greater you!

IT WAS ALWAYS ABOUT THEM. EVERYTHING.
IT ALL REVOLVED AROUND THEM AND THEIR NEEDS.
NOW IT'S ABOUT YOU, THE YOU THAT YOU NEGLECTED WHILE YOU WERE WITH THEM.

THEY USED TO BE THE CENTRE OF YOUR ATTENTION

When you have lived with a narcissist you begin to realise that it is all about them, everything. In order to be with such a person you have to subjugate yourself. Because they are very selfish, if you don't supply them with what they want, on time, there will always be repercussions. You soon start to put your own needs to the back because theirs must come first. If you do start to do things for yourself they will put you down and belittle everything you do. You soon stop doing the things you used to do and give up.

The good news is that once you go no contact with them you get to centre you and start to look after yourself. Over time you will gain confidence about who you are without them. This time it's about you. It is your time to shine.

> YOU ARE NOT BROKEN, YOU ARE HURTING AND IN NEED OF LOVE. THERE IS NO SHAME IN THAT.

YOU ARE NOT BROKEN

The narcissists in your life hurt you, you feel betrayed. You gave your love to someone who could not return it and it hurts. You probably still love them.

Although you feel broken, thinking so can make things worse. Turning around that word broken and admitting you are hurt and in need of love will help you. There is no shame in wanting love but expecting or looking for it from a narcissist is sure to end badly.

They tried to break you and you certainly did succumb to their commands, but look, you can still function. They did not totally succeed.

The narcissist has to be let go of. Continuing to long for their love is destructive and will stop any other love entering your life. You have to rebuild yourself and you do that by starting to love yourself. Taking down the walls of the you they tried to make.

You deserve love, tell yourself this each day. Start with small acts of kindness. If you find it hard to be kind to yourself put an apple in one of your hands and give it to the other hand. Start small and then get big in your kindness. If you can be kind to another like you were to the narcissist then you have the potential to love yourself.

> ERASURE OF A NARCISSIST... WRITE ABOUT THEM. WRITE YOUR STORY EVEN IF IT IS JUST FOR YOU. IN WRITING YOU WILL COME TO THE TRUTH OF HOW BAD IT REALLY WAS. WRITE UNTIL YOUR HANDS HURT, THEN WRITE SOME MORE. WRITE THEM OUT OF YOUR MIND AND LIFE. THEN MOVE ON AND START TO LIVE, FOR YOU.

ERASURE OF A NARCISSIST

All you ever think about is them, even when you leave. They were your main focus while you were with them and even now when they are no longer in your life.

If you write about them every day, how bad it was, eventually you will get very fed up with them. They become boring. You can write in a journal, write your story in a novel or blog about them. However you can do it, just write. Then when you get to that point where you can't write anymore keep writing until the point where thoughts of them cease to make you emotional.

Your arms may hurt, your face may be sore with tears and you feel you can't stop, but you keep at it. There will come a time where it stops, the focus on them, you will feel it. At that time you can lay those ghosts of them to rest and start to focus on you. It can feel selfish at first, self indulgent, after spending a lifetime tending to another's needs, it is not.

Writing is a great way to erase a narcissist. You could even write a fictitious novel and put them in with your roles reversed. You could even make them disappear! However you do it, write and keep writing until you erase them. Then start to live life for yourself.

> AFTER NO CONTACT WITH A NARCISSIST... STOP PEOPLE PLEASING. TRUST YOUR INSTINCTS. OH AND... BE HAPPY! ...YOU ESCAPED.

AFTER NO CONTACT WITH A NARCISSIST

You are forced to change after no contact. Nothing works the same. If you try to carry on as you were you will just attract narcissists again. It is not easy but you have to give up people pleasing. People pleasers are annoying. You will find this once you give it up. You will see in others exactly how you were and how this kind of behaviour got you nothing but abused. It does not work, it just sets you up as a person who is easy to abuse.

It is not easy to give up pleasing others because at first it feels as if you are no longer a nice person. You are still a nice person but now you are a strong, kind person. You don't let others walk all over you anymore, you learn to say no.

You became a people pleaser because you were abused. You tried to appease the abuser in order to try to avoid abuse, yet, you were still abused. The harder you tried the worse it got for you.

Trust your instincts now because they were denied. They could save your life. You were born with instincts, you are similar to an animal. Look at how animals act in the wild, do you notice how alert they are to predators. It is perfectly ok to now start to use that in built, innate awareness that is your birthright.

When you have finally gone no contact don't forget to be happy amidst all your grief, you deserve it. If you managed to leave, what a win. You really are incredibly brave. You actually thought about yourself for once.

ALL THE TIME YOU WASTED ON FAKE FRIENDS WHEN YOU COULD HAVE SPENT TIME ALONE, GETTING TO KNOW YOURSELF INSTEAD.

FAKE FRIENDS

After realising the truth that you are a survivor of narcissistic abuse you may also come to the realisation that many of your friends were also narcissists too. It is a sad truth. All the time you spent with them you now see was false, they used you, made a fool of you. All that wasted time you could have spent being your own best friend instead of neglecting yourself.

You did not see who they were when you were with them. They may have appeared to be very friendly and perhaps that is what you were looking for in a world that didn't understand you or showed any interest in you. The narcissist friends were there showing an interest in you and you were hungry for friends so you went for the bait.

You did not know who they were and when you find out it really hurts. Be kind to yourself. Learn to be your own best friend and it will take away any neediness and hunger you have for either approval, love or company. You may have to stay alone for a while but it will all change, you will be different, a stronger person entering life once again. You will have learned so much, it will give you an edge that others may not have.

> NARCISSISTS WILL INVITE JEALOUSY AT EVERY OPPORTUNITY. THEY CAN'T FORM NORMAL ATTACHMENTS SO THEY USE JEALOUSY TO HOOK YOU INTO AN UNHEALTHY DYNAMIC. BECAUSE JEALOUSY IS SUCH A SHAMEFULL EMOTION YOU THINK IT IS YOUR FAULT FOR FEELING IT, IGNORING THE FACT THAT IT WAS THEY WHO INVITED IT IN.

THE NARCISSIST LOVES JEALOUSY, YOURS!

They will parade in front of you, anyone who has attributes you may not have. In fact, they will invite to your door anyone at all who will collude to bring you down. They will exclude you with their body language, mock you with their laughter and huddle close to the object of their desire, while freezing you out. They do so to ravage your mind so that you will feel insecure and try even harder. Nothing you do will make any difference because they are ill, very ill, sick of mind.

Meanwhile you will be so afraid to show any behavior that will invoke their jealousy because there will be repercussions of abuse. You may find that you can't even talk to another person for fear of reprisal. It is normal to feel jealousy in a close relationship but this jealousy shown by a narcissist can often end in violence and worse. To escape it you have to hide everything you do, say or behave in front of them.

Meanwhile, they are free to do whatever they please in front of you and behind your back. They will create jealous scenarios in front of a group of friends or family to make you appear unstable, emotional and angry, when in fact they are just projecting their own insecurity upon you. Until you leave you may not see the truth of what they were doing.

Build up your self-esteem to make yourself confident instead of insecure and stay away from these game players.

> ANGER CAN BECOME A HABIT HARD TO KICK. IT DESTROYS YOU AND THOSE AROUND YOU. GET ANGRY BUT DON'T STAY THERE. HAVING SEEN HOW NARCISSISTS USE ANGER, COVERTLY AND OVERTLY, MAKE A DECISION NOT TO IMITATE THEM. WHO WANTS TO BE LIKE THEM? NOT A GREAT ROLE MODEL WERE THEY?

ANGER CAN BECOME A BAD HABIT

The narcissists anger can be felt in the air, heard in their voice and seen in their eyes. Their anger, it is theirs, yet we feel somehow that it is caused by us. What did we say or do that was wrong? How did we look the wrong way or even dress the wrong way? It is their anger, they are filled with it. Some of them show it overtly, openly. Some hide it covertly, passively. All of them, no matter what type of narcissist, are angry with the world. You just happened to be near them. It could have been anyone, it just happened to be you.

It would be normal to feel anger at them, after all, they betrayed us. We feel injustice at being abused for just being kind. It all gets to you and you feel angry, but don't stay there, in that anger. Anger will tell you that you need to change, that something is not right and it will propel you to do something. The energy of anger is huge and dynamic but too much of it destroys. If you have been on the receiving end of a narcissists anger you will know what it feels like to be a recipient. It was destructive, it did not help. The only thing it did was control you and that is why anger is often used, to control others by fear.

So the plus side of anger is that it propels you to change. The minus side is that it can be a habit that never leaves you and in the end destroys you and everyone you touch. We want to strive to be the opposite of the narcissist. They tried to degrade us and make us like them, angry, insecure and cruel. Choose to walk the other way. Get angry but don't stay there.

> IF WE HAVE TOO MUCH RAW EMOTION IT MAKES US UNSTABLE. THE NARCISSIST FEEDS ON OUR EMOTIONS, IT IS WHY THEY CHOSE US. BEING EMOTIONAL IS NOT A TROPHY AND NOT BEING EMOTIONAL DOES NOT MEAN WE ARE COLD. IT MEANS WE ARE STABLE.

EMOTIONS ARE THE NARCISSIST'S FEED

Over time, when you have been a victim of narcissistic abuse, you get used to hiding your emotions. So much so that there is often a huge gap between what we feel and how we act. We don't even know how to act anymore. We become stilted and bland, frozen and quiet. Some of us talk too much, eat too much and some get too busy. We are afraid to show any emotion or we get too emotional. However we act is a symptom of trauma. We lost the ability to be ourselves. It is this that we have to regain.

The narcissist chose us because we were empathetic, kind and trusting, *and* emotional. At the time they met us we may have been vulnerable, maybe they helped at a bad time in our lives. They love to see our emotions it is how they get a feed so they particularly like broken, emotional people. They will feign help and appear to be supportive in order to fool you about who they are. They may even provoke you to become more emotional and more unstable.

Learning to be less extreme emotionally is learning to be a more stable person. Someone who is strong enough to be moved by suffering but strong enough to be able to withstand it and not be rendered helpless by it. This is how you help yourself overcome the abuse of a narcissist, by becoming stable.

> JUST BECAUSE THEY ARE NOT VIOLENT DOESN'T MEAN THEY ARE NOT DANGEROUS. COVERT NARCISSISTS CAN APPEAR SHY, SENSITIVE AND VULNERABLE. MUCH HARDER TO SPOT AT FIRST. WATCH OUT FOR THE HARD LUCK STORIES THEY OFTEN USE TO CAPTURE YOU.

COVERT NARCISSISTS ARE HARD TO SPOT

Most people, when they think about a narcissist, will imagine a loud, brash, egotistical person who wants all the limelight and attention. Which makes the covert hard to notice, if that is what your idea of a narcissist is.

The covert narcissist is often shy and quiet. They are therefore a bit of a sneaky type to discover. Some covert narcissists also have a bit of the overt narcissists in them as well, which is even more difficult to get your head around. Not all quiet shy types are narcissists either.

So it is a bit of a minefield when you first start to try to work out how to spot a covert narcissist. What sort of things can you look for?

The covert narcissist will have a veneer of superiority and smug snobbery but, unlike a covert narcissist, they tend not to blatantly say it. If you live with them you can feel it because they look down on you. Everyone is beneath them, so much so that they can't even bring themselves to talk to those below them, you.

They will abuse you or your children behind doors but to the outside world they appear as a paragon of virtue, an upstanding member of the community. It is often difficult to tell others about the abuse of a covert narcissist because it is so hidden. We often hide it from ourselves, blaming ourselves, it must have been something we did to be abused. We have to forgive ourselves because if we didn't see who they were, how could anyone else have see them too? They were in disguise.

> LIES, LIES, LIES...
> THIS IS WHAT YOU WERE TOLD ABOUT YOURSELF. ALL OF IT WAS A LIE TO BOLSTER THEIR OWN LACK OF SELF-CONFIDENCE. ALL THOSE UGLY WORDS THEY THREW AT YOU, REVERSE ALL OF THEM AND MAKE THEM INTO POSITIVE ONES. BE AMAZING!

IT WAS ALL JUST BIG FAT LIES

Everything they said was a lie. The good news is that it also includes everything they said about you that was derogatory. All the put downs, all the jokes were just lies. Now that you know the truth you can't possibly believe any of it any more. All the negative self-talk you do, it can all go, because they put it there.

Turn everything around they said to you and re-write it in a positive form. Claim yourself back from the shell of a human they tried to turn you into.

Everything cruel was a projection upon you of the state of their own lack of self-esteem. They said words to you to take you down and make you feel as bad as them. They only want to reflect the good side of themselves when they look out into the world and they do this by giving you all their bad stuff to wear as if it was yours. Time to evict them from your mind! Liars!

> EACH DAY WITH A NARCISSIST IS ANOTHER DAY OF INFECTION. THEY ARE LIKE A DISEASE CREEPING INTO YOUR BONES, BLOOD AND BRAIN. THEY CAN TAKE YOU TO THE EDGE OF INSANITY AND DEVASTATE YOUR BODY. THEY WILL GIVE YOU AN INVISIBLE DISEASE THAT MAY LAST A LIFETIME. LEAVE WHILE YOU CAN!

LEAVE WHILE YOU CAN

The longer you stay the harder it becomes to leave. Yet we, as victims of narcissistic abusers, often stay a long time because we are so trained. They gaslight us to such a point that we can't leave because they become a part of us, we don't know who we are anymore. Leaving would mean a death of that part of us. It is such a sick relationship on both parts.

The longer you stay the more they will get under your skin. It is even possible that at some point the investment that you made in the relationship will be met with a quick discard of you. They move on pretty quickly once another victim has been found. One that is as pliable as you were to begin with!

These people can make you very sick and the longer you stay the more likely that you will actually get a terrible illness. This sounds extreme yet many survivors are, even after they leave, trying to recover from mental and physical illness. You deserve so much more. Look after yourself, the narcissist will never do that, unless they want something from you in return.

> EVERYTHING HAS TO BE A DECISION, A CUTTING OFF POINT. A TIME TO NO LONGER TOLERATE SOMETHING WE USED TO. ONCE WE MAKE THAT DECISION TO REJECT WHAT WE ONCE ALLOWED TO CAUSE US SUFFERING, IT STARTS TO LEAVE US ALONE. WE WILL STILL ENCOUNTER IT BUT IT NO LONGER HAS THE SAME POWER OVER US.

MAKING A DECISION

It is only when we come to a point of decision that we finally take action. Until that time we waiver. Often a crisis has to be upon us before we move and decide to leave a narcissist. We can get to a point of sheer exhaustion. Our life falls apart and when we get to our lowest point, we say 'enough is enough!'. We make a decision to change ourselves. We can't change them, *ever*. Decision made.

It is not an easy decision to go no contact, not easy before or after but once the decision is made we have to be OK with making it. We have to accept we did that and let it sit with us. Even after we leave we can still have doubts. We may want to return because the pain of not being with them feels worse than when we were with them. This is only selective thinking where we split up the good from the bad and magnify the good, telling ourselves lies.

Once you decide to leave, the decision has been made and should be kept. You can not go back. If you do you will have an even worse time than before you left because, not only will you feel guilty, but the narcissist will use your guilt to punish you further. Make the decision. Stick to it and go the course. Remember the bad stuff, that will keep you away. Write it down in bold somewhere just in case you waiver.

> **IF YOU WERE CAPABLE OF THE GREAT LOVE YOU GAVE TO A NARCISSIST, YOU ARE CAPABLE OF LOVING YOURSELF.**

YOU ARE CAPABLE OF GREAT LOVE

You loved the narcissist in your life so much that it was difficult to get over it. The grief of going no contact with a narcissist or even just ending the relationship seems so much more intense than any other loss you have experienced. It is difficult to explain it to anyone who has not personally been there themselves.

One of the reasons we may have been with a narcissist is lack of self esteem, lack of love. Maybe lack of nurture as a child. Even if you had a good childhood still the narcissist can lure you because you were a kind, caring person, ideal for them.

Because they destroy us so much and on so many levels we leave them with no sense of self, we hate ourselves to the point of destruction. Yet if you think of how much love and care you gave to the narcissist you know that you are capable of love, yet you reserve it for others. You must feel that you are not deserving of love.

The greatest gift you can give yourself after narcissistic abuse, to recover, is a love of yourself that matches any love you gave to another, especially someone who did not deserve it. No one is more deserving of your love than yourself.

> MY REVENGE IS ME! THE ME THAT I RE-BUILT, RE-MODELLED, RE-SHAPED, RE-LOVED. I TOOK APART THE ME THAT YOU HAD TRIED TO MOULD ME INTO. MY REVENGE IS THAT YOU DID NOT SUCCEED!

MY REVENGE IS ME!

My revenge is me, a me I can be proud of. Someone who lived through hell and back and still came out OK. I didn't want to harm anyone even though I felt wronged. What the narcissists in my life did to me felt unjust and it hurt. I can choose to stay hurt or a I can move on. I chose me over them. I decided that I had wasted enough of my life on them.

Instead of falling apart I saw a coming together. Life after the narcissist made me take stock of my life. It was a big wake up call, a call to action. I needed to overcome their abuse. Whatever they said about me or to me was no different to how I felt about myself, they were like an echo.

I left absolutely everything behind and doing so brought on a great loss, a period of profound grief that I felt would never leave. Yet I kept on being strong, then falling apart, strong, then falling apart. Finally I just gave myself a break from life and gave up being so hard on myself. In doing so I saw that I had healed so much and had not even noticed. We can get so busy that we forget to look after ourselves. We hide behind being busy.

I hope that over time you too will find your peace of mind and then when you do, give that back to the world. It is needed now. The narcissist only knows selfishness and destruction, show the world another way. Be you and let that be good enough!

If you have enjoyed this book and gained something from it, please consider leaving a review online to help further my work.

OTHER BOOKS BY ALICE LITTLE

No Contact-the final boundary
A self-help book for the daughters of a narcissist mother, father or family. How to deal with going no contact based on the author's own experience.

Healing from depression
Exploring what caused the depression of the author and how compounded neglect and abuse can lead to mental health issues. With short stories of the author's life explaining her own decent into depression and her transformation and healing. With many useful exercises and advice for the reader.

The story of my life and liberation
In this book the author puts into context the stories within her previous two books describing them as a spiritual journey of transformation and healing.

No contact survivor
This book contains all three of the author's previous books, as above, in one volume. Telling her story of a lifetime of abuse both as a child and an adult, no contact with her family and her healing journey.

Healing the traumatised adult
A book of transformation in which the author explains the methods she used in order to heal herself from depression and suicidal thoughts. With brief stories of the author's life and chapters on scapegoating and awareness of narcissistic predators and their abuse.

Alice Little

Printed in Great Britain
by Amazon